THUNDERBIRDS™

FAB ANNUAL 2004

STEPHEN COLE

CARLTON
BOOKS

THIS IS A CARLTON BOOK

Published by Carlton Books Limited 2003
20 Mortimer Street
London WIT 3JW

Text and design copyright © 2003 Carlton Publishing Group

™ and © 1964, 1999 and 2003 ITC Entertainment Group Limited.
THUNDERBIRDS is a Gerry Anderson Production.
Licensed by Carlton International Media Limited.

www.thunderbirdsonline.com

A CIP catalogue record for this book is available from the British Library.

ISBN 1 84442 992 X

Executive Editor: Roland Hall
Art Direction: Adam Wright
Design: Tony Fleetwood
Production: Lisa Moore

Thunderbirds are Go!

Welcome to the world of International Rescue! My name's John Tracy. I'm normally to be found high above the Earth, in the amazing giant space station Thunderbird 5. From here I can monitor radio signals from all over the world. At the first hint of danger or trouble, I contact my father, Jeff Tracy, the man who created International Rescue and pretty soon my brothers are racing to the scene in those fabulous Thunderbird craft!

But today I'm broadcasting an urgent call of my own – to YOU. International Rescue needs good agents who are always on full alert. This book will help you find out if you've got what it takes! Study the videprints, tackle the challenges, and join me again at the back of the book to check your answers. As ever, I'll be watching out for you!

John Tracy

CONTENTS

Passcode Puzzles

"H-hello, everyone. Everything beyond this point is top secret, so I'm afraid I'll have to ask you for the passcode before you proceed. You can work it out by solving the four puzzles below and writing the right number in the box each time. When you have all four numbers, rearrange them in the code grid to reveal which year in the twenty-first century we at International Rescue live in."

Ship Sums

Each of the Thunderbird craft has a number. Use those numbers to solve the sum below and write the final answer in the box below.

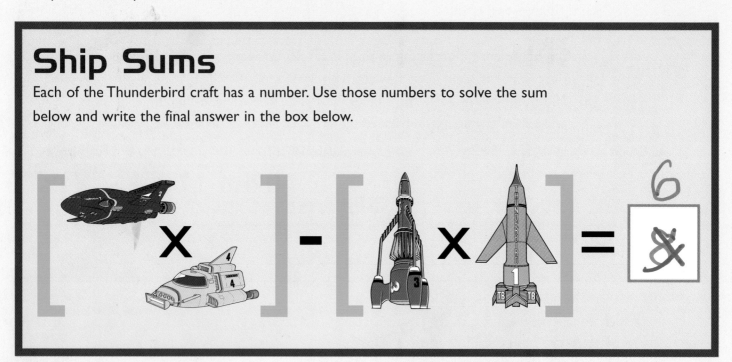

Birth Count

Use the facts below to work out the order in which Jeff's sons were born. Was **John** number one, two, three, four or five? Write the answer in the box below.

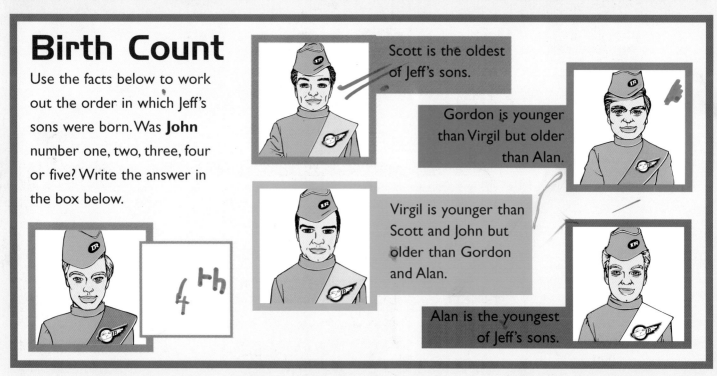

Scott is the oldest of Jeff's sons.

Gordon is younger than Virgil but older than Alan.

Virgil is younger than Scott and John but older than Gordon and Alan.

Alan is the youngest of Jeff's sons.

4 th

Who's That Girl?

The name of a female who's very important to the Tracy household can be found scrambled in the words INTERNATIONAL RESCUE. Who is she? Count the number of letters of her name and write it in the box below.

INTERNATIONAL RESCUE

$\boxed{6}$

Time to Rhyme

Each of the words below can be grouped into rhyming pairs – except one. The last number you need rhymes with the single word remaining!

Hero   Penelope   War   Great

Dot   John   Three   Raw

Eight   Scott   Gone

$\boxed{0}$

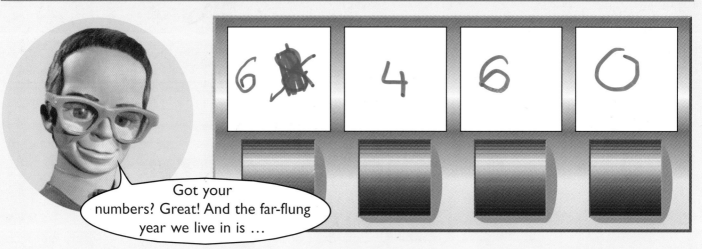

$\boxed{6}$ $\boxed{}$ $\boxed{4}$ $\boxed{6}$ $\boxed{0}$

Got your numbers? Great! And the far-flung year we live in is …

See page 60 for Solutions

REPORT FILED BY:
JEFF
TRACY

"Jeff Tracy here – welcome. Of course, it's always good to see old friends... But when they visit Tracy Island just as an urgent mission for International Rescue is being planned, things can get tricky. I remember one time..."

A NEW AND DEADLY FIGHTER PLANE WAS ON ITS TEST FLIGHT.

PROCEED WITH ATTACK ON INSTALLATION Y!

YES, SIR!

A MISSILE WAS LAUNCHED.

IT SWIFTLY FOUND ITS TARGET...

...TO THE DELIGHT OF TWO SINISTER OBSERVERS, THE HOOD AND GENERAL BRON.

IT IS THE MOST VICIOUS WEAPON I HAVE EVER SEEN!

BUT IN SPEED ALONE, RED ARROW CAN OUTMANOEUVRE US. ALL RIVALS MUST BE REMOVED FROM MY PATH!

I SHALL PAY YOU GENEROUSLY IF ALL PROTOTYPES OF RED ARROW ARE DESTROYED.

LEAVE IT TO ME - THE RED ARROW IS DOOMED!

IT'S NOT LIKE TIM CASEY TO TEST A NEW PROJECT AND MAKE A SLIP. OF COURSE, IT COULD BE SABOTAGE...

EVEN AS I SPOKE, THE SABOTEURS WERE PLOTTING AGAIN.

SOON, RED ARROW 2 GOES OUT ON TEST. IT TOO MUST FAIL!

WHEN THE ENTIRE PROJECT IS ABANDONED, THIS CASKET WILL BE YOURS.

I WILL NOT FAIL YOU, GENERAL! THE GOLD WILL BE MINE!

MEANWHILE...

THERE'S AN UNIDENTIFIED OBJECT APPROACHING, MR TRACY...

...THE PLANE GOT CLOSER AND CLOSER.

HE'S DIVING!

WE'RE BEING ATTACKED!

BUT THE PLANE CAME IN PEACE - CARRYING NONE OTHER THAN TIM CASEY!

GREETINGS JEFF TRACY

THE HOOD'S HOMING DEVICE WAS DRAGGING RED ARROW 2 TOWARDS SKY CONTROL – A TV RELAY TOWER.

GODDARD EJECTED SAFELY INTO THE STORMY SKY...

TWO OPERATIVES, JIM AND STAN, WERE TRAPPED INSIDE THE TOWER'S CONTROL CABIN.

...BUT THE RED ARROW 2 WAS ON A COLLISION COURSE – WITH SKY CONTROL.

THE SIGNAL WAS RECEIVED BY MY BOYS, WHO QUICKLY CLUED ME IN.

WE'VE GOT TO GET OUT THERE AND SAVE THOSE MEN!

MAYBE WE CAN GET THROUGH TO INTERNATIONAL RESCUE!

I SENT SCOTT OFF TO THUNDERBIRD 1...

... AND VIRGIL OFF TO THUNDERBIRD 2 WITH ALAN.

ALL VIRGIL AND ALAN COULD DO NOW WAS WAIT.

WHAT'S KEEPING THESE GUYS?

HERE I GO!

JIM ACTIVATED THE ESCAPE HARNESS AND SHOT INTO THE AIR!

PULL PIN

STAN JOINED HIM JUST IN TIME.

SECONDS LATER, SKY CONTROL CAME TUMBLING DOWN!

LOOK, FELLAS!

Calling Thunderbird 5!

++ TOP SECRET DATAPRINT ++ FOR YOUR EYES ONLY ++
THUNDERBIRD 5 ++ GIANT SPACE STATION IN ORBIT ABOVE EARTH
++ PURPOSE: MONITORS ALL RADIO SIGNALS WITHIN 100-MILLION-
MILE RADIUS ++ SPECIAL FILTERS PICK UP DISTRESS CALLS ++
CONSTANT CONTACT WITH INTERNATIONAL RESCUE MAINTAINED
BY SPECIAL-FREQUENCY ANTENNAE

++ IMAGES ACTIVE++

++ THUNDERBIRD 5 MANNED BY JOHN TRACY
++ AGED 25 YEARS
++ EXPERT IN ELECTRONICS
++ MAXIMUM SECURITY CLEARANCE
++ WHATEVER THE DANGER, JOHN
TRACY KEEPS HIS COOL AND MAKES
SURE PROMPT ACTION IS TAKEN

++ MESSAGE ENDS

Letters by Numbers

Lady Penelope has given Parker a top secret document to deliver to a fellow International Rescue agent. It's been written in a special code. But as an agent-in-training, you have Jeff Tracy's permission to crack the code yourself – using the key below. What does the message say?

KEY	
1=C	2=I
3=H	4=E
5=D	6=S
7=A	8=O
9=G	10=M
11=T	12=P
13=N	14=L
15=B	16=R
17=U	

3 8 8 5   6 2 9 3 11 4 5

7 11   7 11 8 10 2 1

12 14 7 13 11.   15 4

7 14 4 16 11.

3 4   10 17 6 11   15 4

1 7 17 9 3 11   7 11

7 14 14   1 8 6 11 6!

NEXT   BACK   PRINT   LOAD   EXIT

See page 60 for Solutions

Thunderbirds are Go!

When Jeff Tracy formed International Rescue, he knew he would need the most advanced and adaptable rescue vehicles in the world. Well, Brains sure delivered the goods!

We have at our disposal some incredible craft...

SWIFT AND SURE

Thunderbird 1 is a masterpiece of power and control. While it can travel at 15,000 miles per hour, it is responsive enough to interact with vehicles moving at just a fraction of that speed.

HEAVY-DUTY HAULAGE

Thunderbird 2 is so solidly constructed it can withstand fire, collision and other hazards that would cripple lesser craft involved in extreme situations. The pods it carries are also robust – for instance, Pod 4, which holds Thunderbird 4, can simply be dropped from a great height into the sea with no fear of damage to the craft inside.

SPEEDING THROUGH THE SKY

Thunderbird 3's chemical rockets propel it at incredible speed. It can travel as far as the sun in just a few hours, and special shields provide impressive protection from the hazards of space, such as solar flares and meteors.

SPEEDING THROUGH THE SEA

Thunderbird 4 can be equipped to deal with almost any emergency. Here it is carrying a sealing device to cap an eruption of gas from the ocean floor.

THE VITAL LINK

Thunderbird 5 is the linchpin of International Rescue, hovering high above the Earth. Its sensors, receivers and filters are the most sensitive in the world. John and Alan man the space station for a month at a time. It can be lonely work – but if it helps save human lives, it's well worth it!

F.A.B.!

REPORT FILED BY:

BRAINS

"As a scientist, I, uh, applaud any new invention that may benefit the world. But human greed sometimes gets in the way of, uh, true progress and puts innocent lives at risk. I recall one time in particular..."

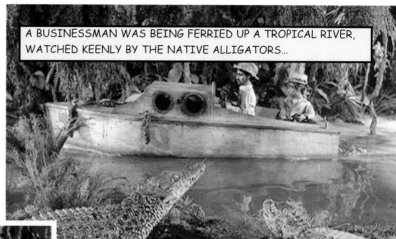

A BUSINESSMAN WAS BEING FERRIED UP A TROPICAL RIVER, WATCHED KEENLY BY THE NATIVE ALLIGATORS...

AT LAST, HE REACHED HIS DESTINATION.

MR BLACKMER, I'M DR ORCHARD, AND THIS IS MCGILL, MY ASSISTANT.

I'D APPRECIATE IT IF WE COULD GET THIS BUSINESS OVER WITH AS SOON AS POSSIBLE.

THE FERRYMAN – CULP – RECKONED THIS 'BUSINESS' MIGHT PROVE MIGHTY INTERESTING.

IN DR ORCHARD'S LABORATORY...

WHAT WE ARE ABOUT TO SHOW YOU, BLACKMER, HAS BEEN TOLD TO NO ONE OUTSIDE THESE FOUR WALLS!

A VERY RARE PLANT THAT GROWS ONLY IN THIS PART OF THE RIVER HAS PROPERTIES THAT WILL ASTOUND YOU!

AS YOU ARE AWARE, THE WORLD IS HEADED FOR A GRAVE FOOD SHORTAGE.

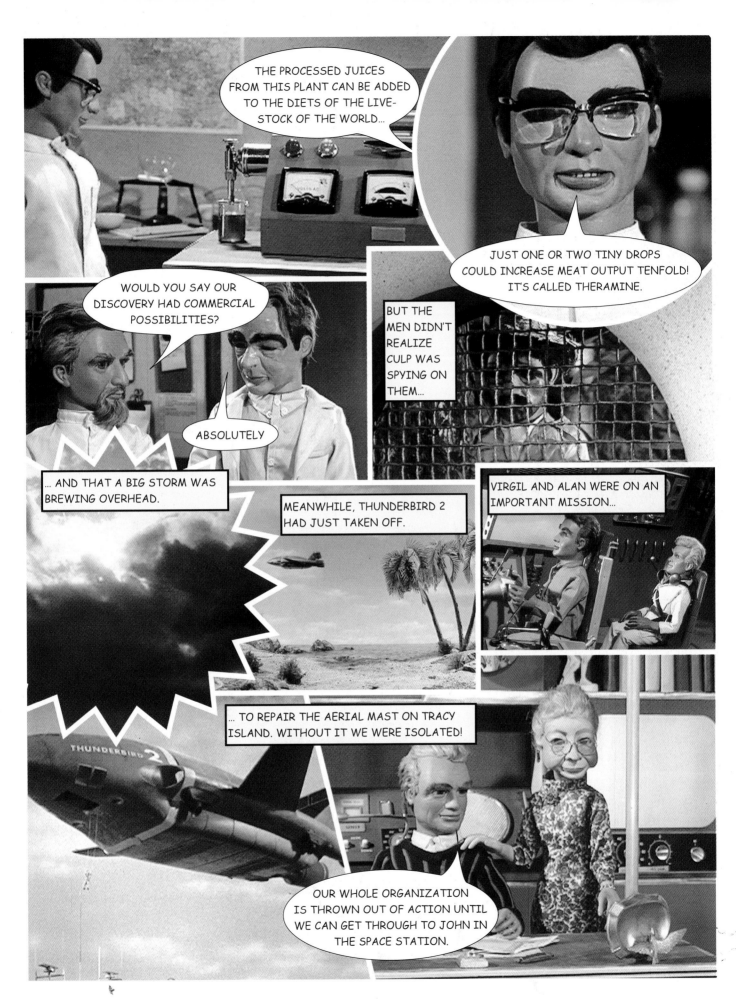

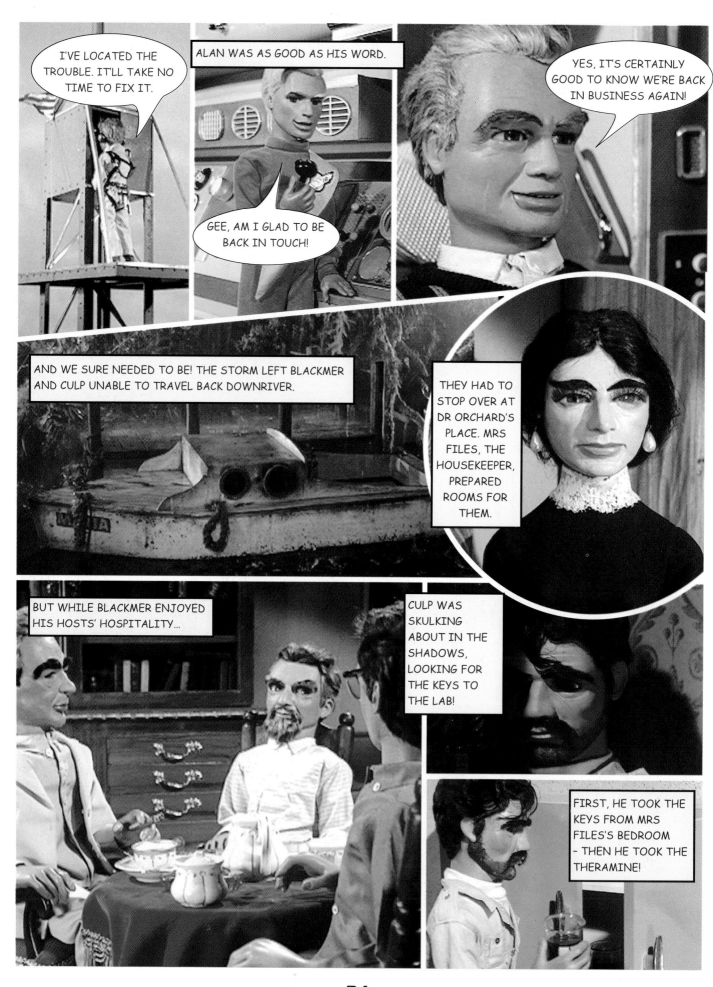

MCGILL JUMPED IN A MOTORBOAT AND SAVED BLACKMER, BUT CULP WAS NOWHERE TO BE SEEN.

THE GIANT ALLIGATORS FOLLOWED THE BOAT STRAIGHT UP TO DR ORCHARD'S PLACE...

...AND BEGAN TO KNOCK IT DOWN!

WHERE CAN WE GO? THOSE BRUTES WILL HAVE THE HOUSE DOWN IN NO TIME!

THE LABORATORY - IT'S THE SAFEST PLACE!

FROM THERE, THEY SENT A DISTRESS CALL TO INTERNATIONAL RESCUE.

IF ANYONE IN THIS WORLD CAN GET US OUT OF HERE, IT'S THEM!

WITH THE AERIAL BACK IN ACTION, THUNDERBIRD 5 SOON RECEIVED THE STRANGE CALL.

GIANT ALLIGATORS?!

26

YOU CAN'T GO OUT, CULP, IT'S NOT SAFE YET!

ALL RIGHT, THE COAST IS CLEAR. I'M GOING TO BE FIRST ON THE MARKET WITH THIS LITTLE POTION!

IF YOUR PALS OUT THERE MAKE ONE MOVE TO STOP ME I'LL POUR THIS COCKTAIL INTO THE RIVER!

SCOTT EXPLAINED THE SITUATION TO VIRGIL, WHO LET CULP ESCAPE WITH THE AMAZING MIXTURE.

SCANT SECONDS LATER, VIRGIL RELEASED THE POD AND GORDON PULLED OUT INTO THE RIVER IN THUNDERBIRD 4...

BETTER STAND BY IN THUNDERBIRD 4, GORDON!

... WHERE HE MADE A VERY BIG DISCOVERY!

VIRGIL! ALLIGATOR!

AS THE REVOLTING REPTILE DRAGGED THE FLEEING CULP INTO THE WATER...

... VIRGIL BLASTED IT RIGHT OUT OF THE WATER WITH A WELL-PLACED MISSILE!

Calling Thunderbird 4!

++ TOP-SECRET DATAPRINT ++ FOR YOUR EYES ONLY ++
THUNDERBIRD 4 ++ ALL-PURPOSE AQUATIC RESCUE CRAFT ++
SUPERB PERFORMANCE IN BOTH UNDERWATER OPERATIONS AND
SEA SURFACE RESCUE ++ EQUIPPED WITH HYDRAULIC RAMS,
DEMOLITION MISSILES, LASER CUTTER, ELECTROMAGNET AND MORE

++ IMAGES ACTIVE ++

++ THUNDERBIRD 4 PILOTED BY
GORDON TRACY ++ AGED 22 YEARS
++ FORMER OLYMPIC SPORTSMAN
++ AQUATIC INVENTOR ++
MAXIMUM SECURITY CLEARANCE
++ INVENTIVE AND CALM BOTH
UNDER PRESSURE AND UNDER
WATER, GORDON TRACY IS A TOP
RESCUE OPERATIVE

++ MESSAGE ENDS

Test Flight Terror

Scott needs your help. A new top-secret plane has run into trouble on its test flight. Too much power is feeding through to its engines. Two of its five power cells must be removed before the plane explodes! Each square power cell is made from nutonium slats held in an energy field. Scott realized that by removing just three slats, he could destroy two of the square power cells, leaving three squares behind. Can you guess how he did it? Use the clear blueprint at the bottom of the page to help you.

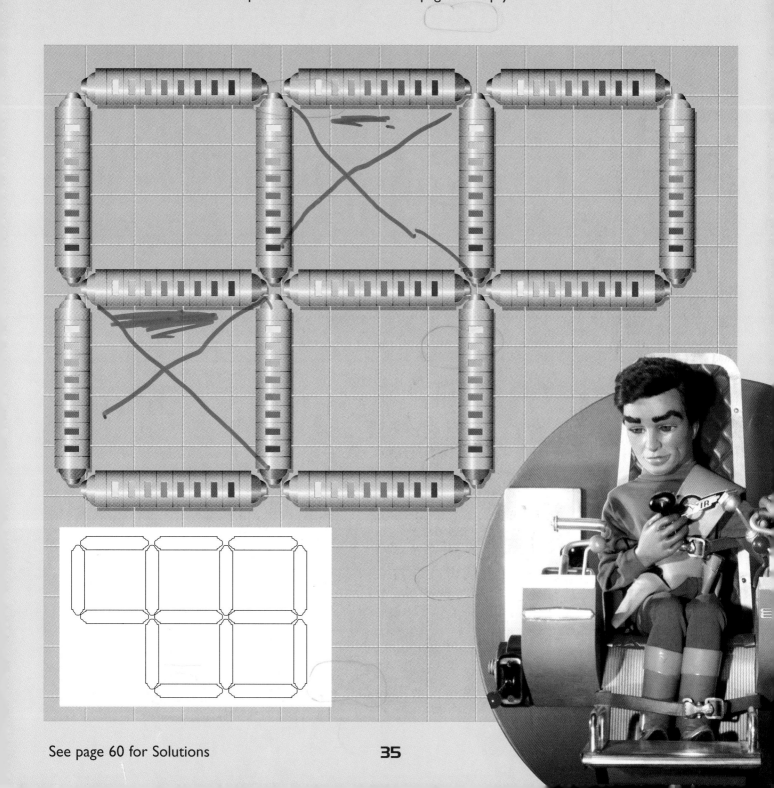

See page 60 for Solutions

Misinformation

Thinking himself the master spy, the Hood has been gathering detailed information on the Thunderbird vehicles, but while some of his information is accurate, a lot of it is wrong! Study each of the statements below. If you think it's true, circle TRUE. Otherwise, circle FALSE.

Thunderbird 2 is a green freighter.
TRUE   FALSE

Thunderbird 4 is carried inside Thunderbird 1.
TRUE   **FALSE**

Thunderbird 3 is designed to travel into the depths of space.
TRUE   FALSE

Not all the Thunderbirds have their numbers stencilled on the side.
TRUE   FALSE

Thunderbird 4 is designed to carry a crew of two people.
TRUE   FALSE

Thunderbird 1 is the
fastest Thunderbird vessel.
TRUE   FALSE

Thunderbird 5 is often
sent first to the danger zone.
TRUE   FALSE

The Thunderbird craft
were created by Brains.
~~TRUE~~   **FALSE**

Calling Thunderbird 3!

++ TOP-SECRET DATAPRINT ++ FOR YOUR EYES ONLY ++ THUNDERBIRD 3 ++ MASSIVE SPACE ROCKET ++ DUAL FUNCTION – PERSONNEL/EQUIPMENT LINK TO THUNDERBIRD 5 AND SPACE RESCUE VEHICLE ++ FITTED WITH TWIN-WALLED HULL FOR METEOR PROTECTION, SENSORS IN NOSE CONE, SPACE-WALK EQUIPMENT

++ IMAGES ACTIVE ++

++ THUNDERBIRD 3 PILOTED BY ALAN TRACY ++ AGED 21 YEARS ++ FORMER CHAMPION RACING-CAR DRIVER ++ EXPERT POTHOLER AND ROCK CLIMBER ++ MAXIMUM SECURITY CLEARANCE ++ DYNAMIC AND IMPULSIVE, ALAN IS AN EXCELLENT PILOT OF MANY CRAFT, AS WELL AS PART-TIME MONITOR ON THUNDERBIRD 5

++ MESSAGE ENDS

Calling Thunderbird 2!

++ TOP SECRET DATAPRINT ++ FOR YOUR EYES ONLY ++ THUNDERBIRD 2 ++ HUGE FREIGHTER ++ TOP SPEED 5,000 M.P.H. ++ RUGGED CONSTRUCTION ++ CARRIES RESCUE VEHICLES AND EQUIPMENT – INCLUDING THUNDERBIRD 4 – TO DANGER ZONE IN ONE OF SIX DETACHABLE PODS ++ WINCH CAPABILITY ++ FITTED WITH DEMOLITION MISSILES, LASERS, DRILLS, MAGNETIC GRABS AND MORE

++ IMAGES ACTIVE ++

++ THUNDERBIRD 2 PILOTED BY VIRGIL TRACY ++ AGED 24 YEARS ++ ADVANCED TECHNOLOGY GRADUATE ++ FINE ARTIST AND PIANIST ++ MAXIMUM SECURITY CLEARANCE ++ DARING AND DEDICATED, VIRGIL TRACY IS ALWAYS WHERE THE ACTION IS, DEVOTED TO SAVING LIVES IN EVEN THE MOST DESPERATE SITUATIONS

++ MESSAGE ENDS

Face It!

Do you know which Tracy brother goes with which Thunderbird? Tin-Tin has scattered images of the boys throughout this grid. Follow the faces up, down, across and diagonally, and you'll find that only once in the grid do the boys' faces follow in sequence the number order of the craft they control – Scott in Thunderbird 1, Virgil in Thunderbird 2 and so on. Work out the complete order and ring the sequence when you've spotted it!

See page 60 for Solutions

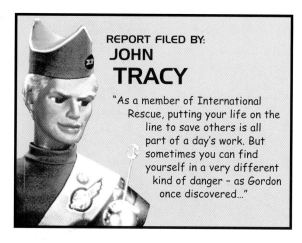

REPORT FILED BY:
JOHN
TRACY

"As a member of International Rescue, putting your life on the line to save others is all part of a day's work. But sometimes you can find yourself in a very different kind of danger – as Gordon once discovered..."

IT BEGAN AS A ROUTINE FLIGHT FOR FIREFLASH 3 – LEAVING LONDON AIRPORT FOR SAN FRANCISCO...

CHIEF CONTROLLER, LONDON AIRPORT HERE, FIREFLASH HAS TAKEN OFF WITH NO MISHAPS...

BUT...

A RESCUE MISSION WAS MOUNTED. THEY SEARCHED BY AIR...

MAYDAY! THIS IS FIREFLASH 3! LOSING HEIGHT RAPIDLY...

... AND BY SEA...

... BUT WITHOUT SUCCESS.

SEARCH NEGATIVE, SIR. FIREFLASH 3 HAS JUST DISAPPEARED!

THE INTERNATIONAL AIR MINISTER WANTED ANSWERS.

ALL FIREFLASHES MUST BE GROUNDED UNTIL THEY ARE CERTIFIED AS AIR-WORTHY.

THAT AIRCRAFT COST NOT ONLY 5 MILLION POUNDS BUT 600 LIVES AS WELL!

ON TRACY ISLAND, WE COULDN'T BELIEVE IT WHEN THE NEWS ABOUT FIREFLASH CAME THROUGH.

WHY SHOULD AN AIRCRAFT LIKE THAT SUDDENLY DISAPPEAR?

DAD CALLED ALAN, WHO WAS STANDING IN FOR ME ON THUNDERBIRD 5.

ALAN, MONITOR ALL TRANSMISSIONS ON THE FIREFLASH TESTS.

WHILE WE PUZZLED OVER THE MYSTERY, COMMANDER NORMAN WAS BRIEFING HIS TEST CREW.

FIREFLASH HAS BEEN CHECKED AND IS IN PERFECT WORKING ORDER.

SABOTAGE?

WITH THE PRECAUTIONS THEY TAKE NOW, SABOTAGE IS UNLIKELY.

I'VE BEEN CHECKING ON THE CRASH. THE FIREFLASH CREW RADIOED A WRONG POSITION. THEY WERE MORE THAN FIFTY MILES OUT!

YOU WILL FLY THE SAME COURSE AS FIREFLASH 3! KEEP IN CONSTANT TOUCH WITH CONTROL.

... BUT NOT BEFORE A MYSTERIOUS FIGURE PARACHUTED FROM THE STRICKEN PLANE!

FIREFLASH STARTED TO SINK - WITH THE PILOTS TRAPPED ON BOARD!

MEANWHILE, THE PARACHUTIST SENT A FLARE FROM HIS INFLATABLE LIFE-RAFT...

IT'S JAMMED! WE'RE GOING UNDER!

... AND WAS PICKED UP BY AN UNKNOWN RESCUE SHIP.

BUT ONCE ALAN HAD PINPOINTED THE FIREFLASH'S TRUE POSITION, WE HAD A RESCUE OF OUR OWN TO CARRY OUT.

SCOTT PUT DOWN THUNDERBIRD 1 ON THE COAST NEAR THE CRASH SITE...

... WHILE VIRGIL LOWERED THUNDERBIRD 2, READY TO RELEASE THUNDERBIRD 4'S POD.

SCOTT, I NEED A COURSE TO TAKE ME TO FIREFLASH'S CRASH POSITION.

STEER 107 DEGREES, MAGNETIC.

GORDON WAS SOON SEARCHING THE DEPTHS IN THUNDERBIRD 4.

I'VE FOUND FIREFLASH! SHE'S IN ONE PIECE!

SUDDENLY, BRAINS CAME UP WITH A GREAT IDEA.

IF YOU CUT OFF THE ENGINES WITH A LASER BEAM, FIREFLASH WILL FLOAT TO THE SURFACE. THEN WE CAN RESCUE THE CREW!

GORDON GOT STRAIGHT TO WORK.

THE FIREFLASH CREW WATCHED TENSELY!

FINALLY, BOTH ENGINES WERE SLICED AWAY...

... AND THE CRIPPLED PLANE FLOATED UP - JUST AS BRAINS HAD PREDICTED!

BUT GORDON'S WORK WASN'T OVER - THE PILOTS STILL HAD TO BE SAVED.

WE'RE ON FIRE!

GORDON SECURED HIMSELF TO THE COCKPIT AND STARTED TO CUT HIS WAY THROUGH.

MEANWHILE, VIRGIL LOWERED A RESCUE CAPSULE, READY TO PICK UP THE CREW.

OK, GUYS, AS SOON AS THE RESCUE CAPSULE ARRIVES, CLIMB ABOARD!

VIRGIL WINCHED THE CREW TO SAFETY...

... AND GORDON CLEARED THE AREA - JUST IN TIME!

MY BROTHERS MADE THEIR WAY BACK HOME - BUT THE MYSTERY WASN'T YET SOLVED!

THE CAUSE OF THE FIREFLASH DISASTERS CAN ONLY BE FOUND WHILE THE PLANE IS IN FLIGHT.

IF ONLY THEY'D LET US FLY ONE OF THEM WITH THUNDERBIRD 2 ALONGSIDE TO HELP IF NEED BE!

HOW ABOUT THAT, FATHER?

WE'LL CONTACT LONDON RIGHT AWAY. IT'S TIME FOR INTERNATIONAL RESCUE TO ACT!

LONDON JUMPED AT THE CHANCE – AND THUNDERBIRD 2 WAS SOON ON THE WAY.

CROSSING THE BRITISH COAST NOW!

SOON, SCOTT WAS SET TO FLY WITH TOP PILOT CAPTAIN HANSON.

ALAN, I WANT YOU TO MAINTAIN CONSTANT CONTACT BETWEEN YOURSELF, THUNDERBIRD 2 AND THE FIREFLASH.

LONDON CONTROL, WE ARE READY TO START TESTING FIREFLASH!

THE AIRPORT WAS CLOSED OFF TO MAINTAIN SECURITY...

... AND THUNDERBIRD 2 TOUCHED DOWN NEXT TO THE FIREFLASH.

ALAN SET UP THE LINKS AS INSTRUCTED, AND THEN...

SCOTT AND HANSON TOOK HER UP. NO ONE KNEW WHAT DANGERS THEY MIGHT FIND.

WE'RE GOING TO HAVE TO RELAY MESSAGES TO LONDON VIA ALAN IN THE SPACE STATION! BUT...

... IT LOOKS AS IF FIREFLASH IS TAKING ONE COLOSSAL CRASH DIVE INTO THE ATLANTIC OCEAN – I JUST CAN'T GET THE NOSE UP!

SCOTT, I'VE SPOKEN TO LONDON – THEY SAY YOU SHOULD BAIL OUT AND LET THEM PICK YOU UP!

BUT THEN WE'LL NEVER KNOW WHAT THE FAULT IN FIREFLASH WAS! WE'LL BE BACK TO SQUARE ONE!

OK, SCOTT. IT LOOKS LIKE WE'LL HAVE TO TRY THAT LITTLE SCHEME WE DISCUSSED EARLIER...

JUDGING BY THE PRESENT RATE OF DESCENT, I'D SAY WE'VE ONLY GOT ABOUT FIFTEEN MINUTES!

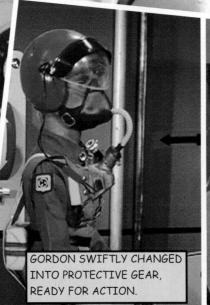

GORDON SWIFTLY CHANGED INTO PROTECTIVE GEAR, READY FOR ACTION.

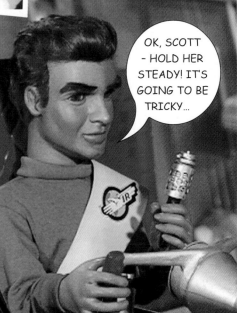

OK, SCOTT – HOLD HER STEADY! IT'S GOING TO BE TRICKY...

VIRGIL STEERED THUNDERBIRD 2 BENEATH THE FIREFLASH'S STARBOARD WING...

... SO GORDON COULD GET INSIDE IT AND REACH THE ELEVATOR POWER UNIT.

FOR A SECOND, AS THE WING HATCH SWUNG OPEN, GORDON THOUGHT HE GLIMPSED SOMEONE INSIDE!

I MUST BE SEEING THINGS!

GORDON ENTERED THE HATCH WITHOUT A HITCH.

TIME WAS RUNNING OUT.

WE'VE GOT LESS THAN FOUR MINUTES!

WHEW! WHERE SHOULD I START?

49

Runaway Reactor

When an atomic reactor went into overdrive, International Rescue was called in. We learned that the reactor's nuclear rods were arranged in an arrowhead, pointing up. To shut down the reactor we needed to rearrange them in an arrowhead pointing down – but we only had time to move three rods! Brains solved the problem in seconds and saved the day. How would YOU do? Can you move just three rods and turn the arrowhead upside down?

This puzzle nearly drove my mechanical marvel Braman right out of his, uh, metal mind!

See page 60 for Solutions

Calling Thunderbird 1!

++ TOP SECRET DATAPRINT ++ FOR YOUR EYES ONLY ++
THUNDERBIRD 1 ++ SLEEK HIGH-PERFORMANCE ROCKET SHIP ++
TOP SPEED 15,000 M.P.H. ++ CAPABLE OF VERTICAL AND HORIZONTAL
FLIGHT ++ DESIGNED TO REACH DANGER ZONE FAST ++ CARRIES
MOBILE CONTROL CONSOLE FOR DIRECTION OF RESCUE OPERATION ++
FITTED WITH DESTRUCTOR CANNON, AUTOMATIC CAMERA DETECTOR,
STEEL SPEARS, REMOTE CAMERAS AND MORE

++ IMAGES ACTIVE ++

++ THUNDERBIRD 1 PILOTED BY SCOTT TRACY ++
AGED 26 YEARS ++ FORMER MEDAL-WINNING
US AIR FORCE SERVICEMAN ++ DEPUTIZES FOR
JEFF TRACY IN CHARGE OF INTERNATIONAL
RESCUE ++ MAXIMUM SECURITY CLEARANCE
++ A QUICK-THINKING, CONFIDENT MAN OF
ACTION, SCOTT MAKES LIFE OR DEATH
DECISIONS WITH PRECISION AND CALM.
HE'S F.A.B.!

++ MESSAGE ENDS

Calling all agents… This is an advanced test designed to prove just how much you know about International Rescue. Study the pictures, write down your answers to the questions, then we will be able to tell if you're an agent extraordinaire or just an average operative!

1 Look at the rescue craft pictured here alongside Thunderbird 1. Is it the Mole, the Domo or Firefly?

firefly

2 What do you think this vehicle is designed to do?

stops fires

3 Who is dressed as Father Christmas in this picture?

Jeff

4 What does Thunderbird 3 travel through when leaving and landing on Tracy Island?

5 What is transported in Pod 4 on Thunderbird 2?

6 What is the name of this evil mastermind?

the hood

7 What is the name of his half-niece who lives on Tracy Island?

TinTin

8 This man sometimes goes by the name of Hiram K. Hackenbacker – true or false?

false

9 To which international airliner does this mighty engine belong?

Thunderbirdz

10 What is Thunderbird 4 doing in the picture – and why?

_____

_____

See page 60 for Solutions

Rescue Plan

A group of geologists surveying an old quarry have crashed their car in an area full of unexploded demolition mines. Virgil can't hover over the area and winch the men to safety – Thunderbird 2's jets could set off the mines!

Scott has decided to take the Mole and tunnel below ground to reach the trapped men. Which set of directions will guide him to the crashed car? Where will the other directions take the Mole?

A) Move 3 squares right. Down 2. Right 2. Down 1. Right 2. Down 2. Left 2. Down 1. Left 1.
B) Move 5 squares right. Down 3. Right 1. Up 2. Right 2.
C) Move 3 squares right. Down 2. Right 2. Down 1. Right 2. Down 2. Left 2. Up 1. Right 1.
D) Move 3 squares down. Right 7. Down 2. Left 2.
E) Move 3 squares down. Right 3. Up 1. Left 1. Up 1. Left 1. Down 1.

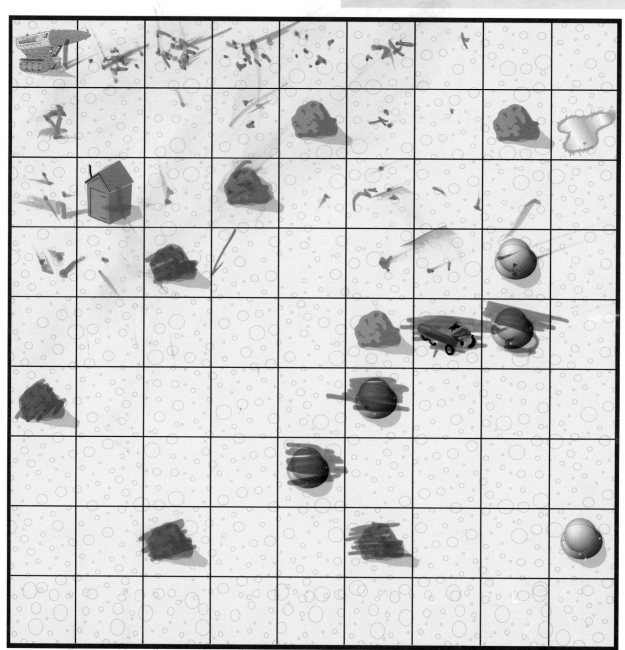

See page 60 for Solutions

International Menace

Lady Penelope is abroad, tracking International Rescue's arch-enemy, the Hood, as he travels from country to country, meeting his evil paymasters. You can follow his trail too! The names of the countries he is visiting are hidden in the grid. Moving up, down and across – but not diagonally – and using each square only once, you must travel from EGYPT and get back again, passing through LIBERIA – TUNISIA – JAPAN – KUWAIT – ALBANIA – GREECE – SPAIN. There is one other country you pass, and that's where Parker and Lady Penelope are hiding!

Start

See page 60 for Solutions

Back-up Squad

The smooth running of our home base means we're able to race to the rescue of anyone in distress in minutes – and that's thanks to three very special people. While they rarely participate in daring rescues directly, without their support International Rescue would be a lot poorer...

++ IMAGES ACTIVE ++

I.R. File 1: KYRANO

++ EXPERT IN BOTANY ++ FIRST BECAME FRIENDS WITH JEFF WHILE WORKING ON A PROJECT TO PRODUCE ARTIFICIAL FOOD FROM PLANTS AT KENNEDY SPACE CENTER ++ YEARS LATER, WHEN JEFF ASKED HIM TO TAKE CHARGE OF DOMESTIC DUTIES ON TRACY ISLAND, HE HAPPILY ACCEPTED – DESPITE BEING PRESTIGIOUS HEAD CHEF AT THE PARIS HILTON ++ HE IS TIN-TIN'S FATHER, AND ALSO THE HALF-BROTHER OF THE EVIL HOOD – BUT NEVER WERE TWO PEOPLE LESS ALIKE!

I.R. File 2: GRANDMA TRACY

++ JEFF'S MOTHER PREFERS TO KEEP HER NAME AND PRECISE AGE CLASSIFIED ++ BORN IN THE LATE 1980S, SHE MOVED TO TRACY ISLAND IN 2065, WHEN SHE OFFICIALLY BECAME A MEMBER OF INTERNATIONAL RESCUE ++ ALWAYS FIERCELY PROTECTIVE OF HER FAMILY, SHE IS A SUPERB COOK, AND HELPS OUT WITH THE DOMESTIC CHORES AROUND THE TRACY VILLA.

I.R. File 3: TIN-TIN

++ A 22-YEAR-OLD WHO POSSESSES BEAUTY AND BRAINS IN EQUAL MEASURE ++ JEFF TRACY PAID FOR HER TO ENJOY AN EXCEPTIONAL EDUCATION IN EUROPE AND AMERICA OUT OF GRATITUDE FOR HER FATHER'S LOYAL SERVICE ++ WORKS HARD ON TRACY ISLAND, FROM ASSISTING BRAINS WITH THE MAINTENANCE OF THE THUNDERBIRD VESSELS TO HELPING GRANDMA TRACY WITH THE COOKING ++ SHE IS ALSO A FULLY QUALIFIED PILOT.

++ BRIEFING SUMMARY
++ LOYAL AND UNSTINTING IN THEIR SERVICE, THESE KEY PERSONNEL ARE JUST AS MUCH HEROES IN THEIR OWN WAY AS THE TRACY BROTHERS!

Special Escort

It is now time for you to leave Tracy Island. You will be assigned a personal escort by one of the International Rescue team. To find out who it is, count the number of letters in your first name. If the number is 6, use it. If the number is more than 6, subtract 4. If it is less than 6, add 3. Now read the chart from the left to right, starting with the top line. The letters which appear with your code number will spell the name of your special escort from Tracy Island!

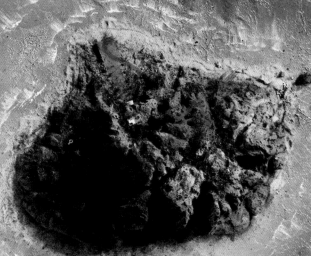

3/G	5/B	8/S	4/A
6/T	3/R	4/L	7/J
8/C	5/R	3/A	6/I
7/E	4/A	5/A	8/O
3/N	7/F	6/N	5/I
8/T	4/N	3/D	6/T
3/M	6/I	5/N	7/F
8/T	5/S	3/A	6/N

AGENT CHALLENGE SOLUTIONS

Passcode Puzzles, page 4

Ship Sums: 4 - 3 + 1 = 2 (2).

Birth Count: John is Jeff's second son (2).

Who's That Girl?: Tin-Tin (6).

Time to Rhyme: Hero (0).

Passcode: The year is 2065

Letters by Numbers, page 19
HOOD SIGHTED AT ATOMIC PLANT. BE ALERT. HE MUST BE CAUGHT AT ALL COSTS!

Test Flight Terror, page 35

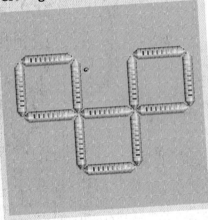

Misinformation, page 36
TRUE – Thunderbird 2 is a green freighter.
FALSE – Thunderbird 4 is carried inside a pod by Thunderbird 2.
TRUE
FALSE – They all do.
FALSE – It is a one-man vessel.
FALSE – Thunderbird 3 needs to travel at 25,200 m.p.h. to reach. escape velocity; Thunderbird 1's top speed is 15,000 m.p.h.
FALSE – It remains in orbit above the Earth at all times.
TRUE

Face It, page 39

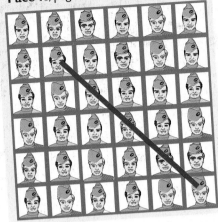

Runaway Reactor, page 52

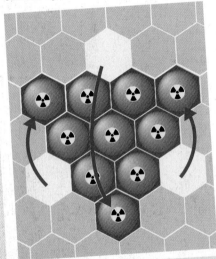

Get the Picture, page 54
1) Firefly. 2) It tackles fires with its powerful heat-resistant shield.
3) Jeff Tracy. 4) The centre of the doughnut-shaped roundhouse.
5) Thunderbird 4. 6) The Hood.
7) Tin-Tin. 8) True. 9) Fireflash.
10) Cutting through the engines so the plane will float to the surface of the sea (see 'Operation Crash-Dive on page 22).

Rescue Plan, page 56
A) This leads you to a mine.
B) This leads you to the pond.
C) This leads you to the crashed car – congratulations.
D) This leads you to a mine.
E) This leads you to the hut.

International Menace, page 57
ITALY

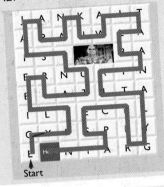

Special Escort, page 59
3=GRANDMA, 4=ALAN,
5=BRAINS, 6=TIN-TIN,
7=JEFF, 8=SCOTT

"Well, I guess it's time to say goodbye for now… From up in Thunderbird 5, I've been monitoring your progress through these pages, and it's clear to me that International Rescue is going to be recruiting a great many bright new agents very soon.

Stay alert… F.A.B.!"

John